Nonnie Talks about Relationships

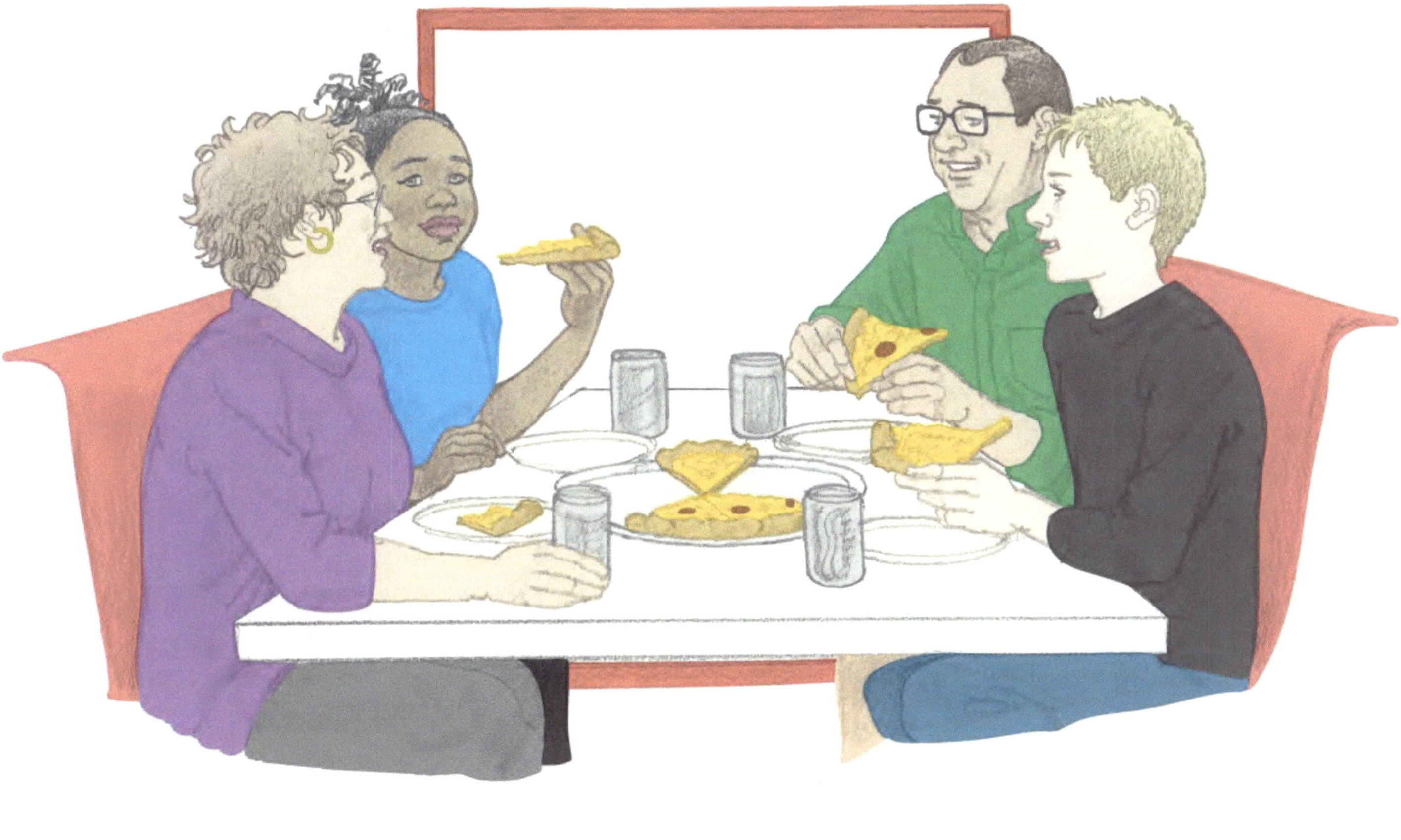

Suggested for children in grades 3-8 and their trusted adults

An Interactive Book for Children and Adults

By Dr. Mary Jo Podgurski
Consultant Al Vernacchio, MsEd
Illustrations by Alice M. Burroughs

One Kid at A Time™

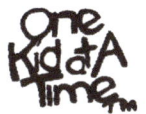

NONNIE TALKS ABOUT RELATIONSSHIPS: VOLUME ELEVEN OF THE NONNIE SERIES

Copyright ©2020 by Dr. Mary Jo Podgurski
All rights reserved

No part of this book may be reproduced in any manner whatsoever without written permission from the author. For information, write AcademyPress, 410 N. Main Street, Washington, PA 15301. The AcacemyPress is the publishing arm of the Academy for Adolescent Health, Inc.

The Academy for Adolescent Health, Inc. website is http://healthyteens.com/

Illustrations created by Alice M. Burroughs are the property of the Academy for Adolescent Health, Inc., and are copyright protected. All rights reserved.

Photographs were purchased for use in this book or were donated and used with permission, for exclusive use in this book.

ISBN-13: 978-1-7343001-2-3

Dedication

Thank you to my generous, wise reviewers:

Nancy Aloi
Isabel Amaya-Fernandez
Dr. Lexx James Brown
Dr. Elizabeth Crane
Joan Garrity
Stella F B Garrity
Mariotta Gary-Smith
Evan Gough
Lily Gough
Bill Taverner

About Consultant Author Al Vernacchio

Al Vernacchio teaches at Friends' Central School in Wynnewood, PA. He is the N-12 Sexuality Education Coordinator and also a member of the Upper School English department. In his work as Sexuality Education Coordinator, Al teaches classes, organizes sexuality-themed programs and student assemblies, provides parent education on human sexuality topics, and is one of the faculty advisors for the Gender and Sexual Orientation Alliance (GSoA).

A Human Sexuality educator and consultant for over 25 years, Al has lectured, published articles, and offered workshops throughout the country. His work has been featured in "Teaching Good Sex", a November 20, 2011 cover story in The New York Times Magazine. Al has given four TED Talks, and has appeared on national programs such as NPR's "Morning Edition", "1A", and "The Pulse". He is the author of *For Goodness Sex: Changing the Way We Talk to Young People About Sexuality, Values, and Health* published by Harper Wave, a division of HarperCollins.

Al earned his BA in Theology from St. Joseph's University and his MSEd in Human Sexuality Education from the University of Pennsylvania. He is a member of The Society for the Scientific Study of Sexuality (SSSS), The American Association of Sexuality Educators, Counselors, and Therapists (AASECT), and Advanced Sexuality Educators and Trainers (ASET). A native Philadelphian, Al and his husband Michael live in the Germantown section of the city.

Introduction: Thoughts about a Child's Developmental Readiness for the Nonnie Series:

Many people ask me for help in determining a child's readiness for the books in the Nonnie Series.

Children today can glean information from online sources in a mouse click or smartphone search, but they are not always as comfortable sharing their concerns with adults. Adults, conversely, may not know how to address complicated topics, or may think a child is "too young" or unaware. I think the power of the Nonnie Series is the message "It's OK to talk about this together" – for adults and children!

Monitor your children's ability to process information. Maturity and age are often unrelated to reading ability; an adult can read and explain complicated words and concepts, but a child's curiosity and eagerness to embrace knowledge are important considerations. Adults need to "articulate the obvious" when educating children. It's important to empower. Try paraphrasing this message: "I'd like to look at this book with you. I think you may be interested in the topic. We can read the book at your own pace. You can talk with me about anything, and I will respect you. I will always respect your feelings."

I suggest grade levels as opposed to age because I'm sensitive to reading ability, but I truly do not feel the books should be limited to one group. For example, not all third- or fourth-graders will be developmentally ready for all the chapters in the books; the books should be read at a child's speed. On the other hand, not all seventh- or eighth-graders will be interested in interacting with an adult to address these topics, but some will enjoy learning and communicating with someone they trust.

No one is more important to a child than a trusted adult. Learning takes place when we process information; communicate with the young people in your life and share your values with respect.

Each child is different. Let your children lead you. Their interest, more than their grade level or age, should be your guide.

Thank you for listening and caring about young people.

With respect and admiration,

Mary Jo Podgurski

Nonnie Talks about Relationships

Suggested for children in grades 3-8 and their trusted adults

By Dr. Mary Jo Podgurski
Consultant Al Vernacchio, MsEd
Illustrations by Alice M. Burroughs

An Interactive Book for Children and Adults

HOW TO USE THIS BOOK:

Nonnie Talks about Relationships was created to be used by children and adults together. Please read this book with someone who matters to you.

For Young Readers:

This picture means you may color the page if you wish.
This symbol * or a red word means a word may be new.
The Glossary on pages 92–97 will help with new words.
Words written in blue are especially important messages or are for you, the reader.

A What do YOU think? page is a great page to help people talk with each other.
Please talk with a trusted adult!
Please listen!

Most important:

Every person is different.
Each child who picks up this book is different.
Each adult who reads this book with a child is different.
Some ideas may be easy to understand. That's OK.
Some ideas may be difficult to understand. That's OK.

©2020~ All rights reserved   AcademyPress ~ http://www.healthyteens.com/

How to use this book:
For Parents, Teachers and Trusted Adults:

1. I strongly recommend reading the book without your child first. Consider any concerns you may have with the material and prepare for your child's possible questions.
2. The book is divided into chapters. The chapters are only suggestions; they divide the content to allow for pleasant learning. The book may be read as one part, two parts, three parts, four parts—it's up to you. You know your children best. Please monitor their attention, their interest, and their awareness and understanding of the concepts.
3. The topic of Relationships is a critical issue in today's world. We all live with connection and relationships. Many young people think the only relationships that matter are romantic or sexual ones. This book seeks to dispel that misinformation; I also hope to aid young people for whom the lack of a relationship can make them feel lonely. Communicate!
4. As Tamika and Alex discuss, relationships, we cover many types. I tried to be as inclusive as possible. I believe each person is worthy. I try to model raising awareness of the real lives young people live.
5. I do focus groups for each Nonnie book. In a Relationship discussion, a 12-year-old said, "Relationships are important, but they don't usually work out." Let's model healthy relationships and communication to our young people. They deserve our best example.
6. Just as children's physical and emotional development are unique, so is their readiness for information. Please let the children you love be your guides.
7. The What do YOU Think? pages should be completed at a child's pace, but are important. Learning takes place when we process information.

Most important:
Be aware of the "music" (tone of voice) behind your words. Adult modeling and acceptance of skills like respect and empathy as an ally are vital.

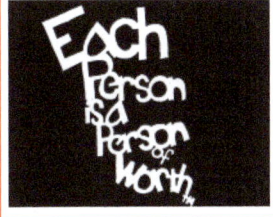

Please teach children the importance of respect.

Mary Jo Podgurski

©2020~ All rights reserved

AcademyPress ~ http://www.healthyteens.com/

©2020, Mary Jo Podgurski, RNC, EdD
Academy for Adolescent Health, Inc.
410 N. Main Street
Washington, PA 15301
1 (888) 301 2311
podmj@healthyteens.com
http://www.healthyteens.com/

Chapter One: The Story Begins

Did you ever have a huge question?

Most children wonder about a lot of different things.

Would you like to read a story
about two children with lots of questions?
The story may answer some of your
questions.

If you still have questions when the story is finished,
please ask your parents or a trusted adult.

Once upon a time….

Alex and Tamika are best friends.

They can't remember a time when they weren't friends.

Their parents said they were even in the same play group when they were only two years old! As they grow older, their friendship also changes and grows.

Alex and Tamika are very curious. When something confuses them or makes them wonder, they often turn to the trusted adults in their families for answers.

They speak with their parents, Tamika's older brother, their aunts and uncles, and their teachers and other trusted adults*.

A trusted adult is someone who respects young people, listens to their thoughts, and keeps promises.

Alex's grandma is a nurse and a teacher and a counselor.

Tamika and he call her Nonnie. Nonnie is the Italian word for grandma. When they're confused or curious about something they often talk with Nonnie. She listens to them, respects them, and helps them grow and learn. She is a trusted adult.

Have you ever wanted to talk with a trusted adult? Who are the trusted adults in your life?

Alex and Tamika are starting 7th grade.

Friendships* are important to them now. They care about what their friends think about them. They remind themselves that Nonnie says what's most important is how they feel about themselves.

They spend a lot of time thinking about how they dress for school and activities. They text and talk on the phone a lot!

Because Tamika and Alex taught their peers* a little last year, they decided they wanted more training as peer educators*.

Peer educators teach and model healthy choices to other young people. Nonnie says, "When an adult teaches young people, the message is heard as a whisper. When a peer educator teaches, it's heard as a shout."

They can't wait to teach. They know Nonnie will answer their questions.

What do YOU Think?

How important are friendships to you?

Do you think you'd like to teach your peers?
Do you like talking in front of others?
How can you be a good role model*?

Please draw or write your thoughts here:

One day, Tamika and Alex had a new question.

An unexpected question.

Nonnie was late for a family dinner!

Nonnie was never late for family gatherings.

Where could she be?

Finally, when the dinner was over, Nonnie arrived.

Alex and Tamika ran to the car to meet her! They were curious. Why was Nonnie late? How did she feel?

Nonnie had taught the children all about feelings.

She said it is okay to feel sad.  Do you ever feel sad?

What do you do when you feel sad?

 It is okay to feel happy. Do you ever feel happy?

What do you do when you feel happy?

It is okay to feel bored.  Do you ever feel bored?

What do you do when you feel bored?

 It is okay to feel lonely. Do you ever feel lonely?

What do you do when you feel lonely?

It is okay to feel mad. Do you ever feel mad?

What do you do when you feel mad?

Tamika and Alex asked Nonnie why she was late.

She was quiet for a long time and then she shrugged.

She said, "I was angry."

"Why?" asked Alex.

Nonnie said, "Because I made a mistake*."

Chapter Two: A Mistake & A Difficult Relationship

The children were surprised. They didn't think Nonnie made mistakes!

Alex thought a moment. Nonnie taught them how to hold space*—how to stay with someone who was troubled, without offering advice. Holding space is giving the gift of your presence* and your time.

Alex said, "We're here, Nonnie. You can talk about it if you want. Or not. It's okay!"

Tamika added. "It really is okay, Nonnie. We love* you."

Nonnie gave them both a sad smile. "I am so very proud of you. But, right now, I'm just angry."

Alex ran to make tea for Nonnie in her favorite china cup.

Then, they sat with Nonnie. It was hard to stay silent. They wanted to know what made Nonnie angry. Nonnie sighed at last. "I trusted someone who did not live up to my trust*. I was fooled by a person who works for me."

Tamika was shocked. Nonnie could usually figure out people.

As if she understood what Tamika was thinking, Nonnie sighed again. "I'm usually able to know if people are lying to me. I got this wrong, though. What a mistake!"

Although very curious, the children didn't ask Nonnie to share and she didn't. After a little while, she began to talk. "I'm dealing with a difficult* relationship*," she began.

Tamika was confused, "You've been married a long time," she said.

Nonnie smiled, but her smile was sad. "I have. It's not my marriage. My relationship with Alex's PopPop is good."

Nonnie sighed again and said, "Thanks for listening, you two. I need to think about this alone."

Nonnie went home.

Tamika and Alex didn't know what to do. Nonnie's problem was confusing them.

Alex said, "We don't know much about our relationships," he said. "How can we help Nonnie with an adult one?"

Tamika had an idea! She said, "Let's call Mr. V."

Mr. V. is the children's favorite teacher.
He teaches Sex Ed*.
He's a person they know will always be there for them.

Mr. V taught them about relationships in his class!

Tamika hesitated. "What if Nonnie doesn't like us asking for help?"

Alex shook his head. "You know Nonnie. She taught us to get help when we need it. I know she'll understand."

Tamika agreed. "She's always telling us to find a trusted adult if we need help. Mr. V. is a trusted adult."

Alex and Tamika thought about their decision. Nonnie always told them they were able to make good choices. They decided calling Mr. V. was a good choice!

They called Mr. V. and he was great. He told them to meet him at the local pizza place and bring Nonnie.

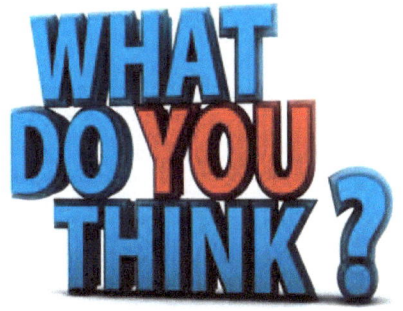

What do YOU Think?

Do you have a trusted adult in your life like Mr. V.?

Do you think Tamika and Alex did the right thing when they connected with Mr. V. ?
Why or why not?

Please draw or write your thoughts here:

The children texted Nonnie:
Nonnie, we talked with our teacher Mr. V. at school. Can you meet him tomorrow?

They were correct. Nonnie was pleased. She understood. As they walked to the pizza place, though, Nonnie was quiet.

By the time they got to the pizza place, they were all three quiet. It's a good thing Mr. V. is able to draw people out and make them feel comfortable. In a very short time, they were laughing!

Chapter Three: Mr. V. , Pizza Help, and Crushes 101

Nonnie thanked Mr. V. for making them feel at ease, and he said, "Pizza helps!" He gently asked Nonnie if she wanted to share her problem.

Nonnie sighed and said, "I hired someone who seemed to really care about young people," she said. "Then I discovered he was lying about spending time with them. He kept notes on his visits, but the notes were not true."

Stunned, the children just stared. Nonnie nodded. "I know. I would never lie about serving young people."

They all smiled. The knew Nonnie would not lie.

Mr. V. said, "Relationships can be complicated* at times*."

Alex snorted. "This isn't a relationship, Mr. V. This man works for Nonnie."

Mr. V. said, "Many people think relationships are only with someone with whom you connect, like a romantic* partner*. The truth is we are in relationships every day with everyone in our lives."

Nonnie smiled at the children and Mr. V. She said, "It is a relationship, Alex. Mr. V. is correct. And, it is complicated."

Alex frowned, "But, relationships are with people you like…ike someone you're crushing on*."

Tamika almost teased her friend. Alex talked about having a crush* on one of their friends a month ago, but not again. She realized this wasn't a good time to figure out his crush, but she made a mental note* to find out more!

Mr. V. smiled. "Can you think of any relationships in your lives?"

Tamika said, "I like my new soccer coach. Is that a relationship?

Mr. V. said a relationship with a coach was an important relationship.

Nonnie agreed with Mr. V. She said, "Alex, can you think about some of the people in your lives.?"

Alex asked, "Like my little sister?"

Nonnie said, "Yes, Alex, your sister Alisha is part of your family. Family members are our first relationships."

Chapter Four: Family Relationships

Alex nodded. "I get that." He thought a moment and then added, "I think my little sister is my favorite family relationship. I love my parents and I love you, Nonnie, but Alisha is…" he paused thinking of words…. "she's fun!"

Tamika agreed. "I don't have a younger sibling*. I do have cousins*, but I love hanging out with Alisha! Remember when we celebrated her first birthday?" Tamika sighed. "She's gotten so big," she said.

Alex laughed. "Now you sound like Nonnie!" He turned to his grandma. "You're always talking about how big I am!"

Nonnie laughed, too. "You're both growing fast. I'm very proud of you," she said.

Alex asked, "Who is your favorite family relationship, Tamika?"

Tamika suddenly looked sad. Alex understood. "Your Abuelito*, right?"

Abuelito is Tamika's special name for her grandfather.

"I miss him so much," Tamika said. "When he lived in New York and I mostly saw him online, I thought I missed him then, but now is much worse…."

Nonnie said, "I remember when you and your family brought your grandparents to California to live with you."

Tamika said, "We brought him here when he got real sick. It was a long flight, but I had fun." Her eyes filled with tears and she asked Nonnie, "How long will I miss him?"

Nonnie opened her arms and Tamika slid right into them. "He will always be part of you. It's OK to be sad," Nonnie said. "It's OK to miss him. You loved your Abuelito a great deal." Alex put his arm around Tamika's shoulders. "He really loved you, too," he said.

When Tamika felt a little better, she wiped her eyes. "I keep reminding myself of when he went home to visit people in the Dominican Republic* I was OK then."

"Why is this different, Nonnie?" she asked, then added sadly, "because he died, I know. He's not just on vacation."

"Grief** and loss are hard because you won't see him again, honey." Nonnie soothed. "When he went on a trip, you knew he would come back to see you."

Alex whispered, "You're my best friend and I love you, Tamika. I wish your Abuelito hadn't gotten sick."

Tamika took a great big breath. "Family relationships are powerful," she said, and nodded her head so hard her hair bounced around her face. "Thanks, Alex. You are a good friend."

*Check out *Nonnie Talks about Death* for more information

Chapter Five: Healthy and Unhealthy Relationships

Then, Tamika frowned. "I can understand relationships in a family or with a coach. What about the lady at the store in town?"

Tamika felt the store clerk didn't trust her, even though she'd never done anything wrong in the store.

"Relationships can also be unhealthy*," Mr. V. said.

Nonnie said, "I agree. Typically, we talk about unhealthy and healthy* relationships when the relationships are close ones, but it sounds as if this clerk isn't treating Tamika fairly."

Tamika said, "My dad told me I can tell if a relationship is unhealthy if a person tells me to lie to my parents. Or, doesn't listen to me and respect me."

Alex added, "My mom said healthy relationships allow each person to grow. And, the people are fair to one another."

Mr. V. looked at Nonnie and smiled. He said, "These are wise young people."

Nonnie agreed.

Nonnie said, "Let's play a game!"

Alex said, "Here?" He looked around the pizza place.

"Yep," said Nonnie. "Right here." She emptied the paper bag she used to carry her purchases from the store. She went shopping before the children met her. She ripped the bag into rectangles* and gave one to each of them. "Fold it like a hot dog," she said. "We're making paper t-shirts."

The children laughed but did as she said.

"Now," she said, "tear the top in a curve." Tamika and Alex looked at each other and shrugged, but they did what Nonnie asked.

"Good," she said, "You've just made the neck of your t-shirt. Now rip a little towards the fold, then turn the paper and rip all the way down the bottom."

They did look a little like t-shirts!

Nonnie said, "I call this game Relationship Hangups!"

Nonnie said, "I play this game at school to teach healthy and unhealthy relationships." She showed them a picture on her phone. "This is one of our peer educators. I ask my students to write all the things that can make a relationship unhealthy on one side of the paper t-shirt. We process and talk about them. Then, we flip over the t-shirts and write the positive ways we can change the hurtful things to make a healthy relationship."

Thanks to peer educator Baylee Hoffaker for the pic!

Tamika and Alex started writing on their t-shirts.

For Unhealthy, they wrote:

Jealous Mean
Lies Pushy
Cheating
Disrespectful
Doesn't Listen

For Healthy, they wrote:

Trusts Kind
Honest Shares
Faithful
Respectful
Listens
Hears

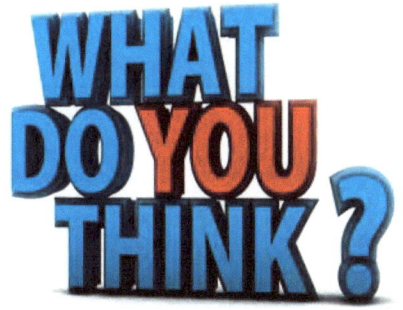

What do YOU Think?

What do you know about healthy and unhealthy relationships?

Write your thoughts about relationships.
Pretend you're playing Nonnie's Relationship Hangups game.
List some other ways relationships are unhealthy.
Then, list some other ways relationship can be healthy.

Please draw or write your thoughts here: ➡

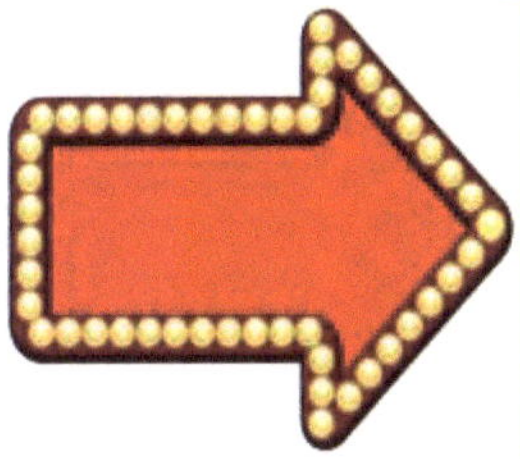

Unhealthy

Healthy

Tamika said, "I liked that game." She paused, then said, "I just never thought about relationships as more than family. Or a boyfriend or girlfriend."

Mr. V. nodded. "Sure. Most people think of the word relationship when talking about a person's sweetheart*."

Nonnie smiled, then said, "Tell us about the clerk."

Alex said, "I don't like the way she treats us when we shop. She follows Tamika around. She never bothers me."

Tamika agreed. "It's like she thinks I'll steal something from the store but I never would."

Mr. V. asked, "Has she ever spoken to you, Tamika?"

Tamika shook her head, "No, but she glares* at me and is right behind me every minute I'm in the store."

Alex asked "Isn't that behavior racist**?"

Nonnie frowned, "Racial profiling* is one way to describe the clerk following Tamika, Alex. You're right, it's not OK."

Tamika said, "So, yeah, some relationships are unhealthy."

Alex added, "So unhealthy…..and just wrong!"

Tamika and Alex looked at each other. Alex said, "I think it's time we do something about this."

Tamika said, "Let's talk with my mom and dad."

Nonnie said, "You two made me think. What my employee* did was wrong. I've known it was. It's time for me to do something about it."

Nonnie thanked Mr. V. They arranged to spend more time with him at his school talking about love* and relationships. They left the pizza place.

*Check out *Nonnie Talks about Race* for more information.

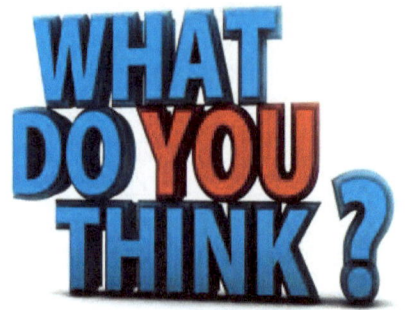

What do YOU Think?

What do you think about the way the store clerk treated Tamika?

Can you think of a time when you knew someone did something wrong? Was it easy to do something about it?

What would you do if you knew someone did something wrong?

Please draw or write your thoughts here:

The next day, Nonnie met with her employee. She told him there were two important guidelines* when she hired him and he signed a contract to serve young people:

1. Connect with young people and give 100% to them.
2. Be honest in all paperwork.

He failed at both things.

Her employee did not admit* he was wrong.
He just turned and left Nonnie's office.

This was a very complicated relationship between an employer* and an employee!

Tamika and Alex went to Tamika's house to talk with her parents about the clerk. She hadn't forgotten when Alex hinted at having a crush on someone.

She started to tease him, asking, "Hey, Alex, who are you crushing on?" Then, she saw the look on his face.

Alex looked confused and a little bit embarrassed*. Tamika reminded herself that her relationship with Alex was a good friendship.

Instead of finishing her thought, she changed what she was going to say. She was respectful of Alex's feelings.

Tamika said, "When we were talking about Mr. V. and Nonnie, you mentioned crushing on someone…."

Alex frowned. "I don't want to talk about it," he said.

Tamika nodded. "When you do, I'm here," she said, even though she was very curious.

Alex was surprised!

Tamika was a good friend!

The truth was, he wasn't really sure who he liked.

Chapter Six: Alex's Crush

That night, Alex thought about some of his classmates. Did he like any of them? No, these friends didn't feel right.

How would he know if he liked someone in a way that was more than friendship?

He liked Tamika, but not *that way*! She was almost like a sister.

He knew he could talk with Nonnie about anything, but...she was still his grandma!

Alex remembered Nonnie said they would talk about relationships and love with Mr. V. He felt better.

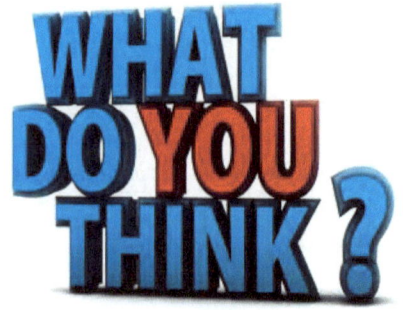

What do YOU Think?

Who do you think is Alex's crush?

Is it OK to like someone as more than a friend?
Why or why not?
What's the difference between a friendship relationship and a crush?

Please draw or write your thoughts here:

Chapter Seven: Relationship Connections

The next day Nonnie, Tamika and Alex went to Mr. V.'s school.
Nonnie asked Mr. V. to help her teach about relationships and love.

Tamika was excited. So was Alex.
Alex wondered to himself, *How do you know if you love someone?*

He didn't ask his question, though. He felt shy*.

Have you ever had a question you didn't ask?
Why didn't you ask the question?

Mr. V. was happy to see them! When they arrived, he welcomed Nonnie, Tamika and Alex. He said, "When I think about any relationship, I like to ask three questions."

Tamika and Alex were interested!

Mr. V. said, "My first question is, *What's the right body to body connection* for this relationship?*"

Alex said, "Body to body?"

Mr. V. said, "Yes, Alex. For some relationships, like with people we don't know well, you don't expect any body contact. Can you think of a relationship like that?"

Alex said, "Sure. The person who mows the grass at school."

Tamika added quickly, "That's one. What about our hall monitor. I smile and wave at her, but we don't touch."

Nonnie asked, "What does your hall monitor do?"

Alex laughed and pulled a picture up on his phone. "She keeps us in line," he said, "but she's really nice."

Alex continued, "I was doing a photo scavenger hunt for photography class and I took this pic of kids running. Our hall monitor was working at the printer, but she slowed everyone down!"

Nonnie said, "Both of those are familiar stranger* relationships."

Alex asked, "What in the world is a familiar stranger relationship, Nonnie?"
Nonnie asked, "Can you guess?"

Tamika said, "Maybe someone we see all the time but don't really know."

"Very close, Tamika," said Nonnie. "You're right about a familiar stranger being someone we see all the time. We also are able to watch them and we don't interact with them."

Tamika wrinkled her nose, thinking. Alex said, "The hall monitor is a familiar stranger to me, but not to the boys she caught running in the halls!"

Tamika laughed. "They had to interact with both her and the principal," she said.

Mr. V. said, "There are also casual* relationships that can happen in life but do not involve love.

Nonnie agreed, "There can be different kinds of body contacts in casual relationships, right, Mr. V.? A work relationship may include a handshake, but not a hug."

Mr. V. agreed. "And, friends often hug," he added. "They don't need to touch to be good friends, though."

Alex asked, "What if the relationship is more..?"

Nonnie understood.
Alex was trying to figure out his crush. Tamika got it, too. She said, "If you have a sweetheart, your body contact would include hugs and kisses...and maybe some kind of sexy stuff!"

Alex punched her arm lightly, and Tamika just grinned.

"What about families?" asked Tamika. "My grandma is a big hugger!"

Alex glanced at Nonnie, "So is mine," he said, smiling.

Nonnie added gently, "Each family is unique*. Body to body connection would also include a higher level of touch in most families, too. Right?"

Alex said, "I love hugging Alisha and she hugs me." He thought a moment, then added, "I learned to only touch when she gives consent*, though. If she says, stop tickling, I stop!"*

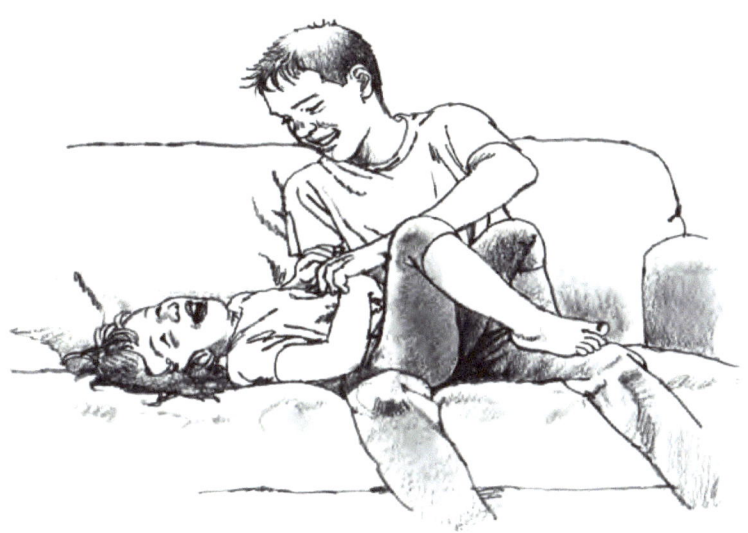

Tamika agreed and said, "Nonnie, your friend Dr. Lexx taught us consent for touch is always important."

Mr. V. and Nonnie were pleased.

Alex was anxious to talk about more. "What are your other two questions, Mr. V.?" he asked.

Mr. V. said, "My next question is *What's the right heart to heart connection* for this relationship?*"

Tamika said, "I like this question! I bet it's about love."

*Check out *Nonnie Talks about Consent* for more information.

Mr. V. smiled. "When we talk about hearts, we often mean love, but I'm thinking about another type of connection. An intimate* connection."

Alex frowned. "We talked about intimacy* before, right, Nonnie?"

Before Nonnie had time to speak, Tamika said, "We did! Intimacy is sharing our truest thoughts and feelings with another person." She looked at Nonnie, "Right?"

Nonnie looked so proud of the children. "That's part of it, Tamika," she said.

Mr. V. added, "When we are intimate with another person, we show them our real selves. We share our hopes and fears."

Alex said, "I know an intimate relationship. Your papa and mama, Nonnie. My great-grandparents."

Nonnie smiled. "A great example, Alex," she said.

"Good friends can have strong heart to heart connections, too, right?" Alex asked, looking at Tamika.

"True," said Mr. V.

Tamika fake growled, "Yeah, but you won't share your crush with me…." She laughed. "I know someone who is crushing on you," she began, but the look on Alex's face made her stop. Alex looked mad.

Mr. V. said, "We all need privacy, even with high heart to heart connections. We don't need to share everything with another person!"

Tamika sighed, "Sorry, Alex. I guess some secrets are OK!"

Alex just nodded.

Nonnie said softly, "Relationships are built and maintained and need trust. My employee broke the trust in our relationship."

Alex said, "And, the relationship ended."

"It did, Alex," said Nonnie. "I wish I'd known about his behavior sooner."

Tamika asked, "If you have a romantic partner or a sweetheart and trust is broken, do the people split? We have friends who just broke up."

Mr. V. said, "Yes, Tamika. Relationships end for many reasons."

Tamika thought about it. "I want to be careful when I start a relationship," she said. "What's your third question, Mr. V.?"

Mr. V. said, "My last question is, *What's the right mind to mind connection* for this relationship?*"

Tamika said, "I like this idea. I like thinking of connecting mind to mind!"

Mr. V. said. "Another word for this connection is commitment*." He smiled at the children. "I think you two have a very high mind to mind connection."

Both children beamed!

Nonnie said, "They do! They also work hard to keep their relationship healthy and strong!"

Mr. V. nodded. "In every relationship, we get the chance to say 'yes' or 'no' to the relationship every day. In a successful relationship, people find a way to say 'yes' to their relationship every day."

Nonnie said, "This is so helpful, Mr. V. - can you explain the thermometers* on your whiteboard?"

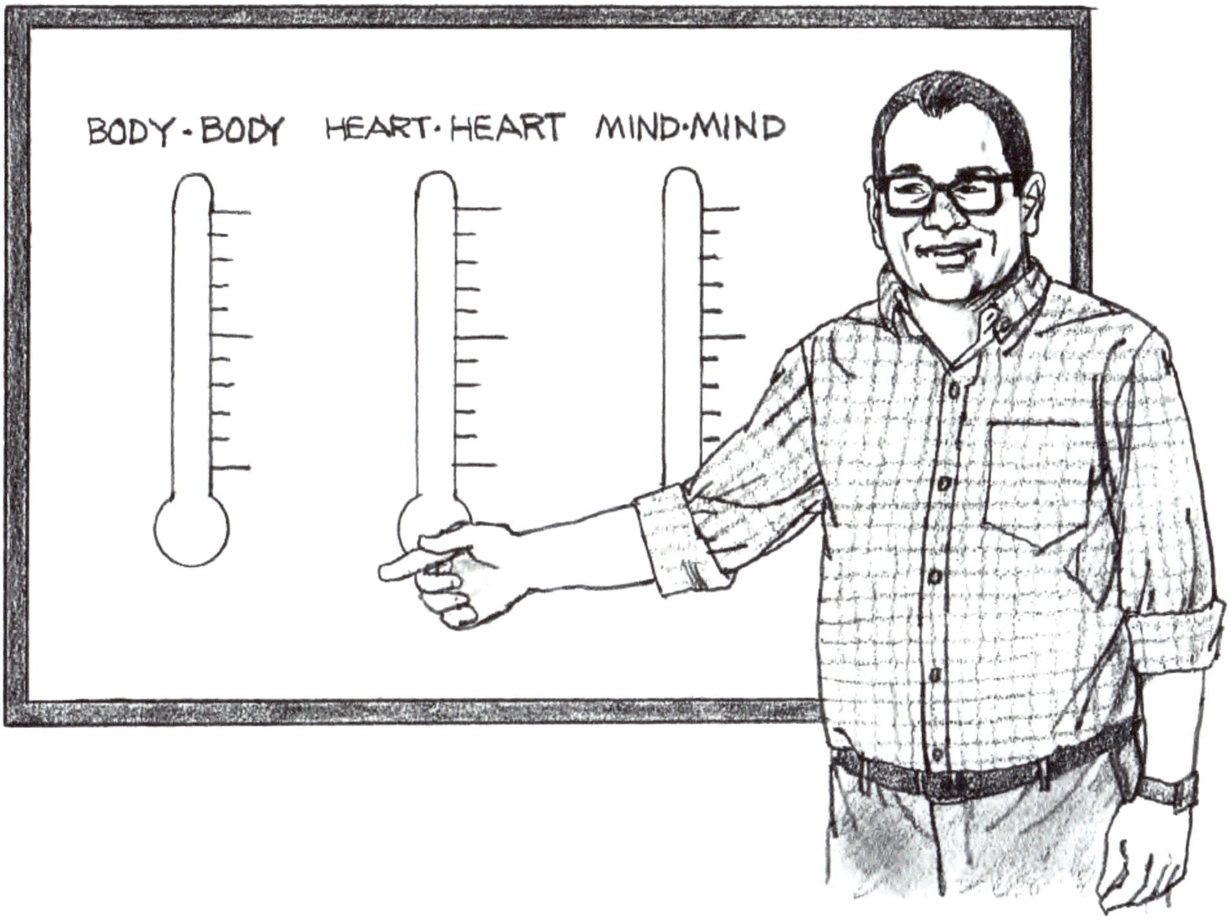

"Sure," Mr. V. said. "I use them to talk about 'taking the temperature'* of a relationship."

Tamika said, "This kind of sounds like a game!"

"It is, in a way," said Mr. V. "Give me an example of a relationship and we'll take its temperature."

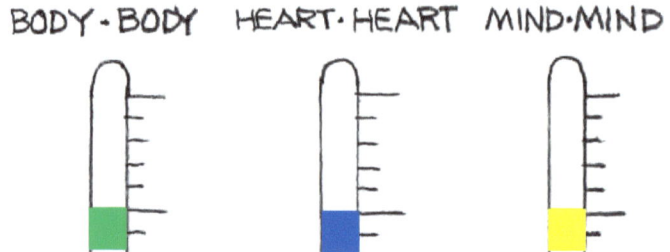

"The store clerk," said Alex.

Tamika spoke quickly. "With her, my body to body connection is low, my heart to heart connection is low and my mind to mind connection is low."

"How about us, Tamika?" Alex asked.

"Our body to body connection is pretty low," she said.

Alex said, "Yep. Just a hug once and a while. But our heart to heart connection is pretty high."

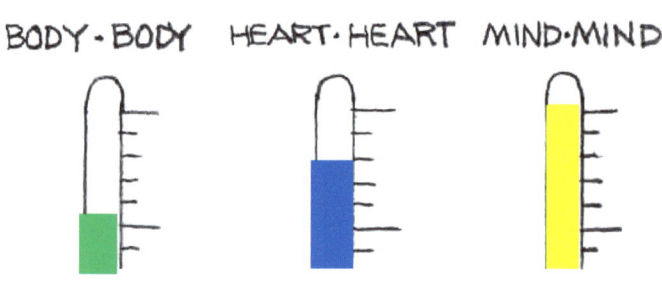

Tamika said, "And our mind to mind connection is very high."

"What about….a…." Alex began, and Tamika said gently, "a crush or sweetheart?"

"What do you think?" Nonnie asked.

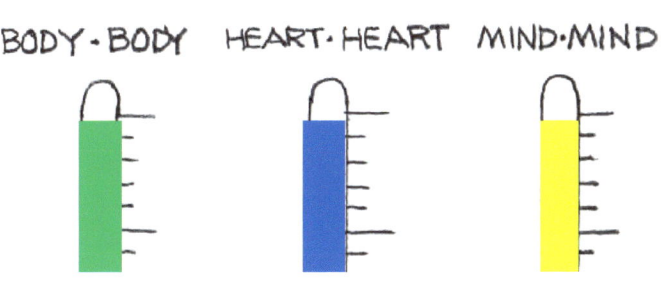

Tamika said, "I think all three connections would be high when you have a sweetheart."

Mr. V. said, "When we have a crush on someone, we work to develop a closer physical (body to body) and emotional (heart to heart) connection with them."

Alex asked, "How do you work at connection?"

"Through communication*, Alex," Nonnie said.

While Mr. V. was talking, Alex started daydreaming.

He pictured more classmates.

Did he like any of these classmates in a way that was more than friendship?

No, none of these friends seemed right.

Then, Nonnie started talking about attraction*.

She said attraction happened when feelings are different than friendship. She said attraction didn't always mean love. She reminded them of Mr. V's thermometer.

The feelings may be romantic (including when you want someone to be your sweetheart and do romantic things together) or sexual* (when you imagine kissing someone or doing something sexy together).*

Alex was still not sure!

Deciding who he liked as a friend was easy!

Deciding who he was attracted to was much harder.

Alex decided not to think about it at all!

He knew Nonnie would tell him to face his worries, but it felt easier to just pretend it wasn't a problem.

*Check out Nonnie Talks about Sex…& More for more information.

Chapter Eight: Listing Relationships!

Have you ever put a thought that worried you out of your mind to try to forget it? How did you feel if you did?

Did you share how you felt with anyone? Do you think you should share? Why or why not

On the way home from Mr. V.'s school, Nonnie took the children to the beach.

They walked together quietly. The ocean sounds were comforting.
Nonnie knew Alex was worried.

She didn't push him to talk.

She didn't force him to look at her.

She just walked along the beach with Tamika and Alex.

They both wondered what was on Nonnie's mind.

After a little while, Nonnie sat down in the sand with the children.

She said, "I'd like to talk about relationships with you."

Tamika and Alex sat beside her. Tamika said, "OK."

Alex frowned and said, "Don't we already know lots about relationships?"

Nonnie said, "We've talked about some types of relationships, but not all."

She asked the children to write in the wet sand.
"List all the important* relationships in your life," she said.

Tamika leaned over and wrote love in the sand.

She giggled and teased Alex. "Alex is in love," she said in a sing-song voice.

Alex blushed* and looked angry, until Nonnie said, "Being in love is a wonderful thing" and both children looked at her.

"I'd love to see your lists," she coaxed.
These were the children's lists:

Alex
1. My Family
2. Tamika
3. Nonnie
4. My dog
5. ?

Tamika
1. My Family
2. Alex
3. Nonnie
4. My friends
5. My coach

Both the children grinned when they saw each other's names in the sand.
Nonnie was pleased to be on their lists!

Before Tamika could tease Alex, Nonnie said, "You're brave, Alex. Listing a question mark makes you vulnerable*.

"What's vulnerable, Nonnie?" asked Tamika.

Nonnie asked, "What do you think? Being vulnerable is connected to being in a loving relationship."

Tamika said, "Ummm...maybe...if you love someone, you could be hurt."

"Exactly!" said Nonnie. "I love you both, so I am vulnerable. If something happened to either of you, it would make me very, very sad."

Alex said, "I forgot to list my coach. I would be sad if she wasn't my coach."

Nonnie smiled. "You both forgot to list a lot of people." Nonnie opened her phone and went to her pictures.

"I'm going to show you some pics I took to show your little sister, Alex. I am teaching her about our community." Nonnie showed them the photos.

She said, "What do you think? Do you have relationships with these people?"

Chapter Nine: Casual Relationships & Connections

"That's not our school," said Tamika. "We don't wear school uniforms."

Nonnie agreed. "I snapped this picture near your house, Alex."

Tamika said, "I like our bus driver. She's very kind. I think that's a low body-to-body relationship."

"This picture is from the culinary* school near my office," Nonnie said. "This is one of my former students."

Alex shook his head.

"We have a casual relationship with the people who prepare our food." He grinned. "Except at home. Which reminds me, Nonnie. You need to make us some of your meatballs real soon."

Nonnie laughed and said she word. Then she asked, "Is Alex correct, Tamika? Do we have serious relationships with the people who prepare our food?"

The children thought about Nonnie's question.

"Maybe only if we know them," Tamika said.

"But we should respect* them and the way their work makes our lives better," said Alex.

Nonnie smiled and showed them more pictures.

Alex said, "I like that waiter. He's at our favorite restaurant." Nonnie nodded. "These are my friends, so I could take their picture with their permission."

Tamika looked at the next picture and laughed. "The fireman with the red beard is funny," she said. Alex agreed. "He came to our school and told jokes."

Nonnie grinned. "I've heard him teach children. He uses humor* to make his students feel okay. He and his partner talk about fire safety and he wants everyone to be relaxed and have fun."

Nonnie showed them more pictures from her phone.

Tamika said, "I remember those workers! They were building a new house near your place, Alex!"

Nonnie nodded. "Do you know these people?" she asked.

"I do!" Tamika said.
"Me too!" said Alex. "They're the cleaning crew at our school!"

"True," said Nonnie. "What are their names?"

Tamika and Alex just looked at her.
"Their names?" Alex was confused. Tamika was, too.
She said, "Why would we know their names?"

Nonnie said, "Because they're people of worth, just like us. One of my questions on the final exam I give my college students is, 'What is the name of the person who cleans the halls?'"

Can you name some casual relationships in your life?

Nonnie said, "Every time we meet someone, we have a chance to be respectful and show people they are worthy. They may be casual or even familiar stranger relationships, but we are all interconnected."

She showed them one more photo before they left for home. "I asked a photographer friend to photoshop this image," she said. "I'm using it in a workshop about communication and connection. Do you see what I mean?"

Tamika said, "I think you mean we're all connected."

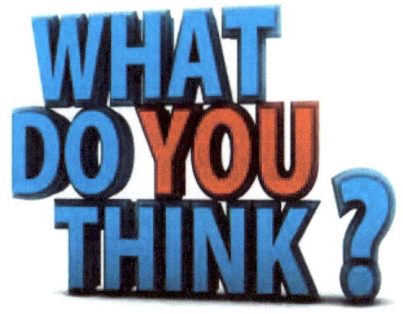

What do YOU Think?

What do you think of Mr. V.'s teachings about love and relationships?

Do you love someone in your family?
Do you know someone who has a crush on another person? Do you think it is OK to have a crush?
Why do you think Alex is confused about his crush?

Please draw or write your thoughts here:

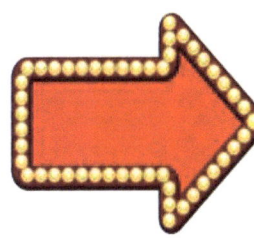

Chapter Ten: Other Relationships in our Lives

Next weekend, Tamika and Alex walked to Nonnie's house. They wanted to check in on her and make sure she was feeling okay about her experience with her past employee.

When they arrived, Nonnie made them a nice Caprese salad* with vegetables from her garden.

While they ate, Nonnie talked about relationships again.

"Tamika, you talked about your coach," she said. "You both have good relationships with your coaches. Do all of your friends connect well with their coaches?"

Alex frowned. "No," he said, sadly. "There's this one coach who is mean."

"I know which coach," Tanika said. "If his team losses, he's angry at the players."

Nonnie agreed. "A mentor* teaches by words and example," she said. "Adults make mistakes. When you see an adult acting poorly, learn what not to do when you're a grown up."

Nonnie smiled and asked, "Can you think of any other relationships beyond friends, partners and family?"

"My dentist," said Alex. "I like my dentist*. She's nice."

"My doctor," said Tamika. "My doctor makes me feel safe."

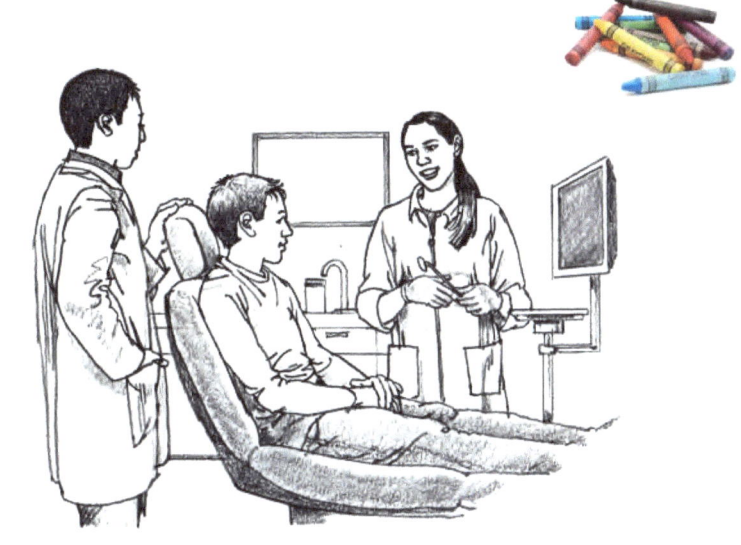

"My doctor is my friend Avian's doctor, too."

Nonnie agreed. "We do have relationships with our health care providers*." Nonnie said, "A counselor* or therapist* is another type of helping relationship."

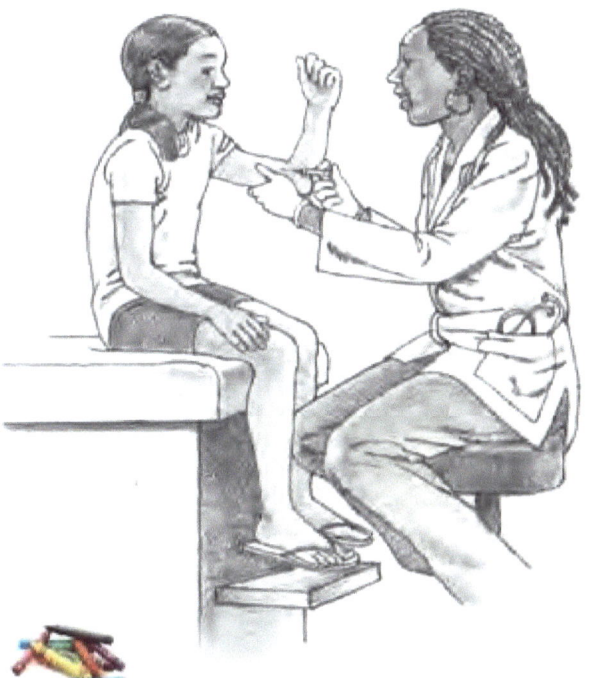

"Wait a minute," said Tamika. "I have a relationship with my piano teacher!"

Alex said, "I have a kind of relationship with my sister Alisha's dance teacher."

 Tamika was shocked! She said, "What! Is she your crush? Alisha's teacher is way too old for you."

Alex laughed. "No way! It's just that I wait with Malik every week to pick up our little sisters and…"

"And…." Tamika prompted…

"Well, a few weeks ago, Alisha's dance teacher asked us to dance with the little ones in a number for their recital."

Tamika beamed. "Are you learning to dance? That is so cool!"

Alex grinned. "It is cool. I'm learning a lot. I like it!"

Nonnie smiled, "I love the way you two support each other. Can you think of any other relationships?"

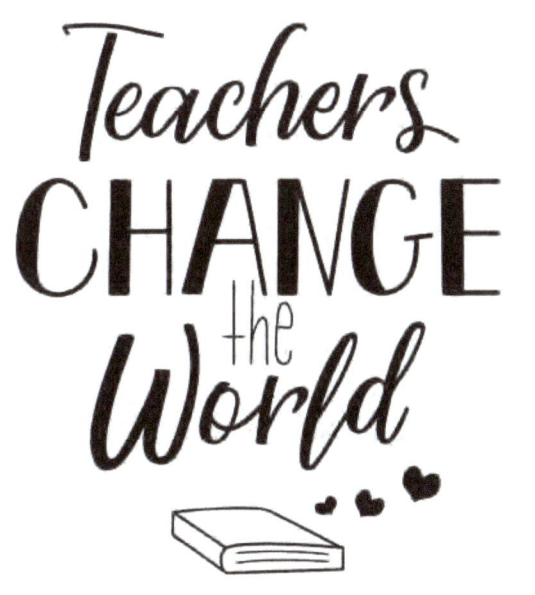

Tamika said, "Alex made me think. We have other teachers besides the adults who teach us music and dance. We have our school teachers!"

Alex said, "Our teachers are always there for us. Like Mr. V."

Tamika laughed. "Our principal is there for us, but she's pretty tough!"

Both the children remembered when their families met with Ms. Kean about them misusing their phones! Alex sighed, "She was right, though."

Nonnie was proud. "It's not easy to admit mistakes. I had to do that this week," she smiled. "You both helped."

Alex said, "Being a peer educator means we create our own teacher—student relationships."

Tamika thought a moment. "How about my minister*?" she asked. "He's almost part of my family."

Nonnie agreed. "Yes. Faith leaders* can be important relationships. Do you have any relationships like that, Alex?"

Chapter Eleven: Relationships with Faith Leaders

"I do," said Alex. "Remember, My mom is Jewish* and my dad is Christian*, so I need to study both faiths."

Tamika grunted, "Sounds like a lot of work, Alex."

Alex shook his head. "It can be confusing. My rabbi and my pastor are pretty chill, though. They know I study with them both, and they're just interested in me being happy and okay."

"Any other kinds of relationships?" Nonnie asked, pleased.

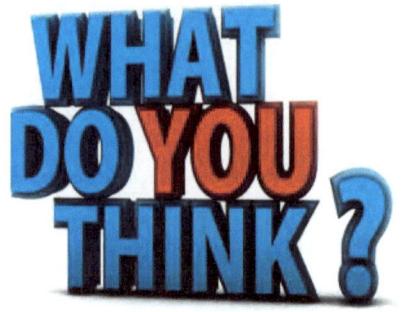

What do YOU Think?

A person can have many types of relationships.

Name some relationships in your life.
Are they casual relationships or do you spend a lot of time with these people?
What is your best relationship?

Please draw or write your thoughts here:

Chapter Twelve: When Relationships Fail

Alex frowned, "Maybe. Could we talk about families? Mine feels a little messed up."

Nonnie knew Alex's story, but, since he didn't talk about it often, she settled back and listened.

"My mom and dad had trouble getting along," Alex said. "When I was five, they went to a relationship counselor*, but they told me they couldn't make it work."

Tamika asked, "What does that even mean?"

Nonnie waited until Alex sighed, "My dad said they both still loved me, but they no longer loved each other. So they separated*."

"Divorce*," Tamika whispered. "Nonnie, do you remember our friend Annie? Her parents are getting a divorce."

"I remember Annie," Nonnie said. "Divorce can be tough. How is she?"

"Not so good," said Tamika. "Her parents fought over her. Annie called it custody*."

"Custody can be difficult," Nonnie said, "It happens when two people are separated but both want to raise a child."

Tamika nodded, "Annie needs to spend every other weekend with each parent and a couple of weeks each month she stays with her dad and he drops her off at school. He doesn't live near our school any more."

Alex was quiet. Nonnie wondered what he was thinking.

Alex seldom talked about his parents' divorce.

Nonnie patiently waited to see how he would react.

Tamika added, "Annie texted me yesterday, Nonnie. She asked if you would talk with her."

"Of course," Nonnie said, watching Alex.

Tamika added, "Annie's life is really a mess, Nonnie. Her dad has a new partner with three kids!!"

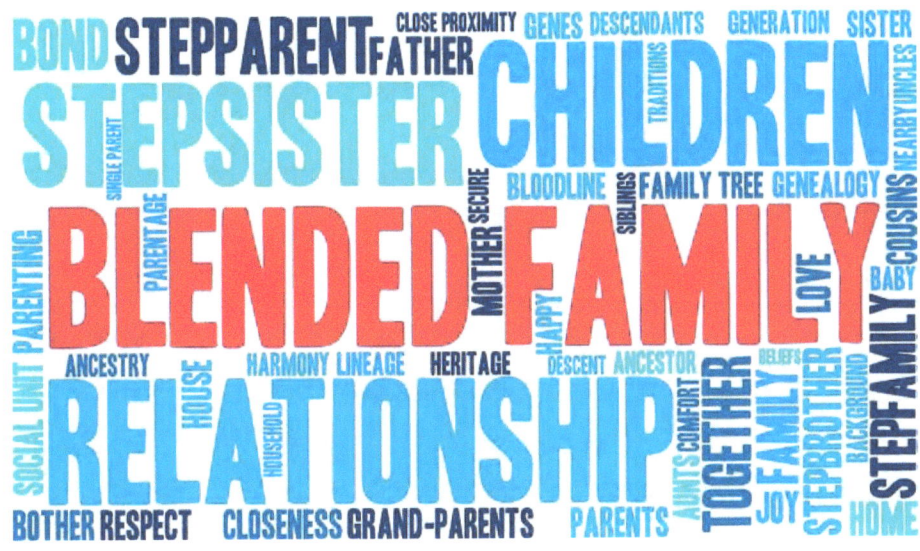

Nonnie said, "When two families come together because the adults start a new relationship, the families need to make new connections. This is called a blended family*."

Tamika frowned. "Why do I think that's not always easy?" she asked. She glanced at Alex. He was still quiet. "Are any of our friends part of a blended family, Alex?" she asked.

Alex shook his head.

Both Nonnie and Tamika knew Alex was having trouble sharing his feelings. They waited patiently.

Finally, Alex sighed. "I remember when my dad married my stepmom. I was pretty upset. I didn't like her at all at first. She wasn't my mom."

Tamika said gently, "Your stepmom didn't have any kids, though, so it wasn't like a blended family. Right, Nonnie?"

Nonnie smiled "In some ways," she said, "You were small when your dad brought your stepmom home, Alex."

Alex looked at Nonnie. "I remember spending lots of time at your house." He grinned. "Lots of popcorn and late night movies and playing board games."

Nonnie grinned. "We had fun. I was younger then," she added gently. "I do remember. It was a sad time for you."

"You're okay now, though, right, Alex?" Tamika was worried about her friend.

"Mostly," said Alex. "I love my stepmom now. I wouldn't have Alisha without her. And my mom and dad are often together. They told me they decided they were still my parents and they would do all they could to make my life good."

He paused, thinking. "The wedding day was hard for me, though. I was only six. I didn't like my dad that day."

"Why do people break up, Nonnie?" Tamika was curious.

"Why do you think, Tamika?"

Tamika said, "Maybe they just grow apart."

Alex mumbled, "Maybe one of them cheats."

Nonnie said, "Cheating* can mean trust is lost."

Alex suddenly smiled. "Remember when we taught a lesson about trust as peer educators, Tamika?"

Tamika said, "I do! I love teaching others!"

Alex said, "Nonnie, when two people have trouble in a relationship, do they always break up?"

"No, Alex," Nonnie said. "Some relationships are strong enough to get past problems."

"What if the problem is about someone breaking trust?" Tamika asked.

Alex spoke first, "I think relationships might end because its too hard to fix the relationship after trust is broken."

Tamika said, "When I'm ready for a real relationship, I want to start with trust and respect."

Nonnie was pleased. She asked them to write all the things they hoped for in a relationship with a romantic partner on her small whiteboard. They began with trust.
What would you write?
Start with trust….

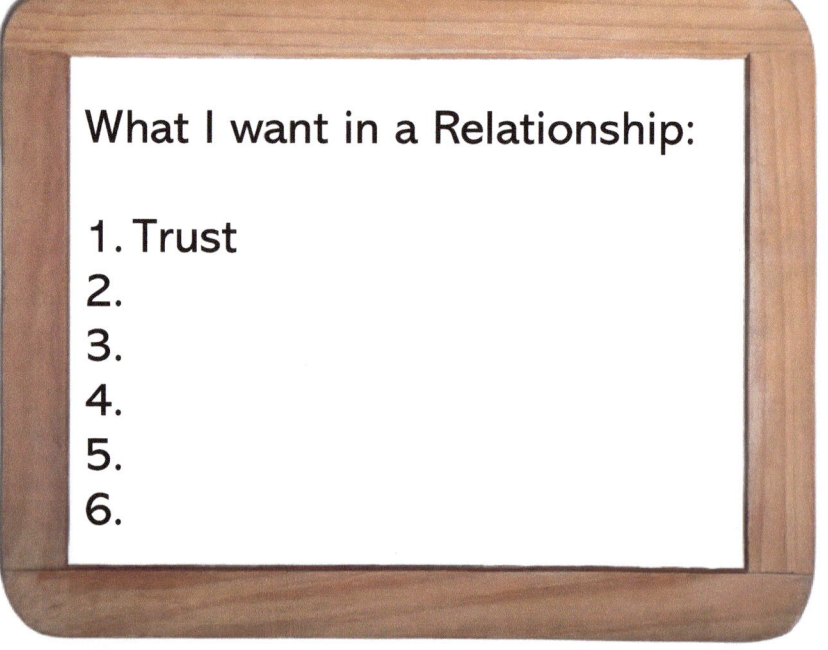

What I want in a Relationship:

1. Trust
2.
3.
4.
5.
6.

Nonnie looked at their lists.

Tamika wrote:
Respect each other
Enjoy sports
Like to have fun
Be honest

Alex wrote:
Read books & talk about them
Laugh together
Share things
Know when to be quiet

Nonnie was pleased. She thought Tamika and Alex were starting to know what a healthy relationship looks like.

Tamika frowned. "Nonnie," she said. "There's so much drama about relationships in our school. People say they're in love but they're are always breaking up."

Alex said, "Maybe they weren't in love at all."

Tamika frowned. "Yeah," she said. "You know what makes me mad?" she asked. "When people ghost you."

Nonnie was confused. "Ghost? Like at Halloween?"

Tamika said, "Ghosting* is like when people don't text back."

Alex said, "I'm tired of talking about love. I have questions about families."

What do YOU Think?

Divorce can be difficult for young people. At first, Alex didn't like his stepmom. Break ups can be tough for people of all ages.

Can you think of a time when an adult relationship changed your life? Do you feel comfortable talking about the change? Do people in your school talk about relationship drama?

Please draw or write your thoughts here:

Chapter Thirteen: All Kinds of Families

Alex asked, "Why are people so mean about different types of families, Nonnie?"

"Can you help me understand your question, Alex? Are you talking about someone you know who is mean to a friend and your friend's family?"

"Yes," They both said. Tamika and Alex looked at each other the way they did when they know what the other person is thinking.

Alex said, "Our friend Hailey has two moms. Just last week, a kid from school texted her and said some really awful things about her parents."

"How is Hailey feeling, Alex?" Nonnie asked.
Alex said, "Mad. Confused. Sad. Lots of feelings."

Nonnie sighed. "You two are amazing young people. We've talked about some very serious* things as you've grown up. Do you remember when we talked about racism with my friends Marti and Renee?"*

Tamika and Alex remembered. Alex said, "We talked about when people don't respect others because of their race or skin color." He looked at Tamika. "And, I learned how to be a good ally."

"Good. I'm glad your remember our conversations," Nonnie said proudly. "I think some people are mean to those of us who are different from themselves."

Tamika said, "I don't get it. Hailey's moms are white."

*Check out *Nonnie Talks about Race* for more information about racism.

"They are," said Nonnie, "but Hailey's moms are lesbian*, and some people say hateful things about gay* or lesbian people."

Tamika shook her head, "I still don't get it. People are just people."

Alex said, "Each person is a person of worth, right?"

Nonnie said, "I believe so, yes."

Alex thought and added, "There's a new kid at school. I heard someone teasing him about having two dads. Same idea."

Tamika said, "We need to be strong allies, Alex. When we hear someone putting him down for his family, we must speak up." Alex agreed.

Nonnie added, "Remember to model acceptance*. People may say they tolerate* differences in others. I tolerate broccoli*!" The children laughed. Nonnie said, "I believe people are worthy of acceptance, not just tolerance."

Nonnie said, "Families are different for other reasons, too. Can you think of any?"

Tamika said quickly, "There's a family at our church that just adopted* their son from foster care*."

Alex said, "My friend Steven was adopted when he was a baby."

Nonnie said, "Adoptive parents take children to be their own. There are many reasons for adoptions. Sometimes a family cannot have babies. Other times, a family wants to raise children who are already born."

Tamika asked, "What's foster care? I know about adoption."

Nonnie said, "Children are placed in foster homes* when their own families cannot care for them. Foster parents help raise them. Sometimes a foster family will adopt a foster child."

Tamika nodded, "I think that's what happened," she said.

Nonnie said softly, "No one picks their families."

Tamika said, "My mom tells me and my brother how lucky we are. She works with children who aren't safe in their own families."

"What do those children do, Nonnie?" Alex knew his parents loved him. He didn't pick his stepmom to be part of his family, but he grew to love her. He had a hard time imagining a family where he didn't feel safe.

"What do you think?" Nonnie said.

Tamika and Alex looked confused, so Nonnie asked, "Who matters most to you?"

"Our friends," Alex said quickly.

Nonnie nodded. "You've created your own small family. A word for that is kin*. Family isn't just the people to whom we're born."

Tamika grinned and poked Alex, "You're part of my family," she said.

Alex smiled back. "And, you're part of mine." He looked at Nonnie. "Does that make us kin?"

Nonnie said, "What do you think?"

Both children said, "Yes!" then Tamika added. "Our parents are kind of a tribe together, too. I remember us getting together since we were small."

She suddenly got sad. "I remember when your parents divorced, Alex," she said kindly. "You didn't just spend a lot of time at Nonnie's house, you slept over at our place a lot."

Alex nodded, but he was quiet. Tamika and Nonnie looked at each other. Nonnie said softly, "Children may blame themselves when adults split up. It's never a child's fault."

Alex mumbled, "I know that."

Tamika asked gently, "But, do you believe it?"

Alex looked at her. "Most of the time," he said with a sigh.

"My mom and my dad and my step-mom tell me that all the time." Alex said. Nonnie said, "You both have great families."

Alex shrugged and said, "I can think of another type of family. Kendle's mom is a single parent*."

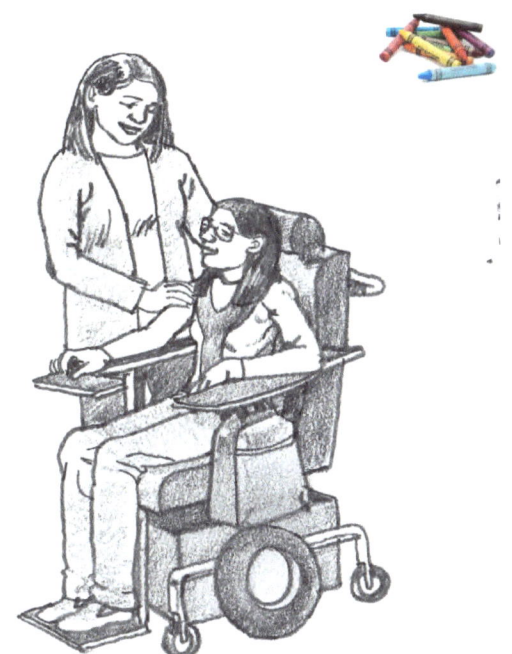

Tamika was surprised. "How did you know that, Alex?" she asked.

Alex mumbled, "I go to her house and hang out once and a while." Tamika didn't say anything, but she was curious.

"Great conversation about families," Nonnie said. "Can you think of any other relationships?"

Tamika made a face like she just ate a lemon. "Friendships - they're messy."

Alex said, "We're friends. We've been friends since we were little kids."

Tamika snorted. "We're not messy. But, my school friends are." Alex knew what Tamika meant. She shared things with him.

Chapter Fourteen: Friend Relationships

"You're talking about fake friends*, aren't you, Tamika?" he asked.

Tamika nodded. "I've been friends with Juli since kindergarten. All of a sudden, she leaves me out of stuff. Has overnights and doesn't invite me. Talks behind my back."

Nonnie said, "Friendships can be very hard if they change*. Change is almost always a challenge anyway, but losing a friend can be a difficult change."

Tamika looked angry. "I would never lie to someone," she said. "Juli is so nice to my face and so mean otherwise."

Alex said, "That must be tough."
Tamika smiled at him. "It is. It helps you're there."

Nonnie sighed. "Relationships can be complicated. I teach an educational psychology* class at the college. I use a book called *Odd Girl Out* about relational aggression*."

"Relational what?" asked Alex. "Relational aggression happens when people are hurt by relationships," Nonnie said.

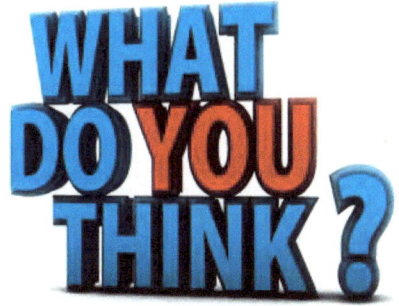

What do YOU Think?

Families are all different.
Friendships can change.

Draw a picture or write a word picture about your family.
List the people in your family and talk about your relationship with each one.
Talk about the idea of fake friends.

Please draw or write your thoughts here:

"Like bullying*, Nonnie?" Tamika asked.

"In some ways. When a person is bullied," Nonnie said, "someone says or does mean things to another person, over and over, on purpose."

"Like being made fun of," said Alex. "Or called names."

"Or cyberbullying*. When people bully online or on phones and tablets," added Tamika.

The children were quiet. Nonnie waited. Finally, Tamika said, "I think making new friends is hard."

"How do we make new friends, Nonnie?" Alex asked.

"There are lots of ways," Nonnie said, "but one of the best things to remember is to be yourself."

Tamika nodded. "Because if you're not yourself, people will never get to know the real you."

Alex said, "Tamika, we really have lots of good friends." Tamika sighed, "Maybe I should stop worrying about being friends with people who are fake!"

Nonnie said, "Let's think about your friends. What do you like about them?"

Alex said, "I like how we laugh together."

Tamika said, "I like our adventures."

Alex smiled. "Remember when we went to the city on the subway with David and LaShauna?" David and LaShauna were peer educators they met at the Teen Center.

"That was fun," said Tamika, grinning. "Those are good friend relationships."

Alex agreed.

Chapter Fifteen: Attraction

Alex grew quiet. He was thinking.
He imagined more classmates. He knew Tamika and David and LaShauna were good friends but he didn't have a crush on any of them.

He didn't think of Hailey or Dylan or Annie or Malik as more than friends.

"Nonnie," Alex said. "Can we please talk about attraction?"

Tamika felt Alex's confusion. "Yeah," she said. "Like how do you know when you're attracted to someone?"

Nonnie got out her big whiteboard and markers. "Good idea. Let's talk about attraction," she said. "You're at a very good age to talk about it."

"Why?" asked Tamika.

"Because you're in the middle of puberty*. Many people have crushes and first romantic relationships in puberty."*

Tamika clapped her hands. "I love whiteboards!" she said. She grabbed a purple marker and started writing.

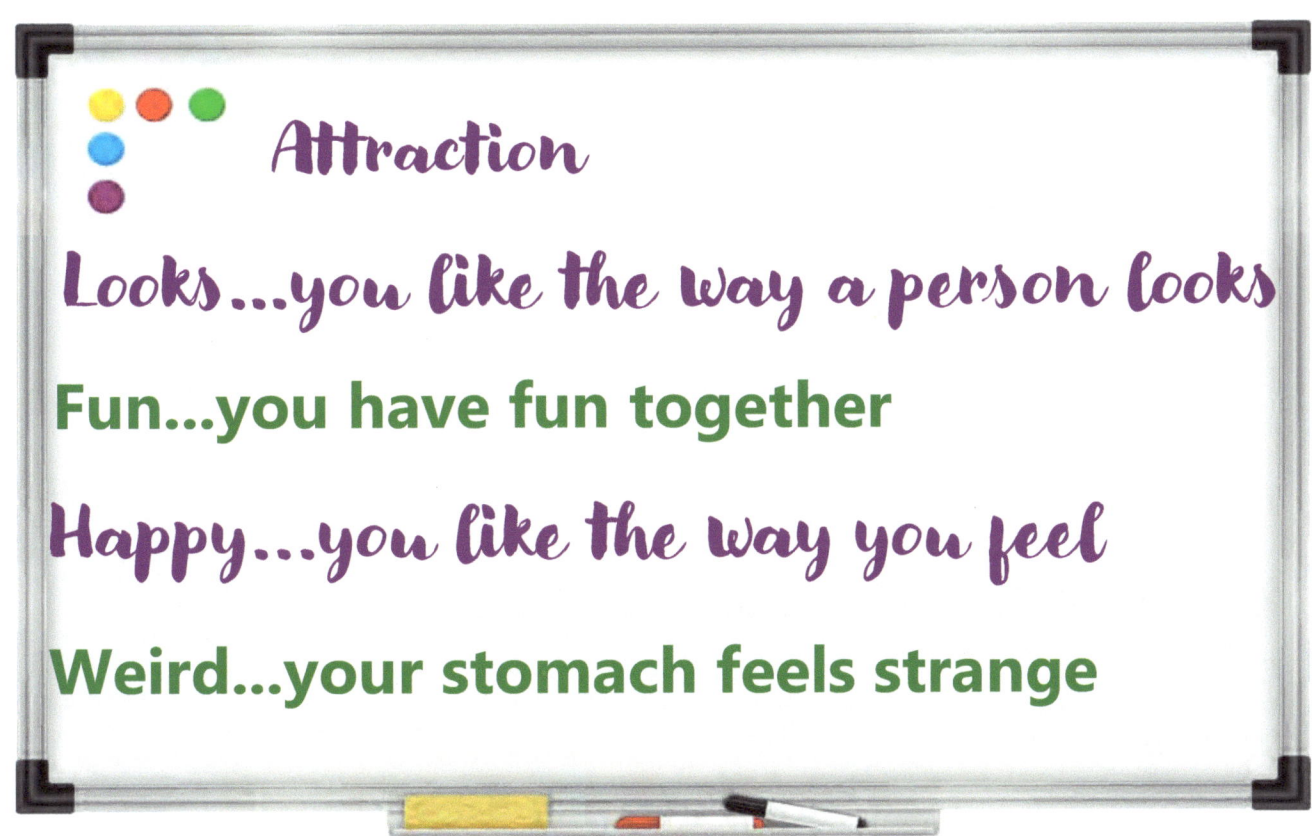

They took turns writing. Alex used a green marker. Nonnie watched and nodded and smiled.

*Check out Nonnie Talks about Puberty for more information on growing up.

Tamika asked Alex, "Your stomach feels strange?"

Alex was restless. "Let's go ride our bikes."

Tamika shook her head. "Not yet." She turned to Nonnie. "Why would Alex's stomach feel weird?"

Nonnie smiled. "When two people are attracted to each other, physical things may happen to their bodies. Do you want to know more?"

Both the children said, "Yes," quickly.

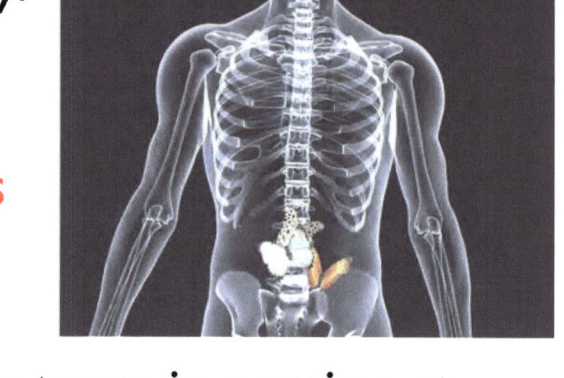

Nonnie said, "What Alex is describing is often called butterflies in your stomach*."

"Like when I'm goalie and the other team is coming at me fast!" said Tamika.

"A little like that," said Nonnie. "Your hands can be sweaty."

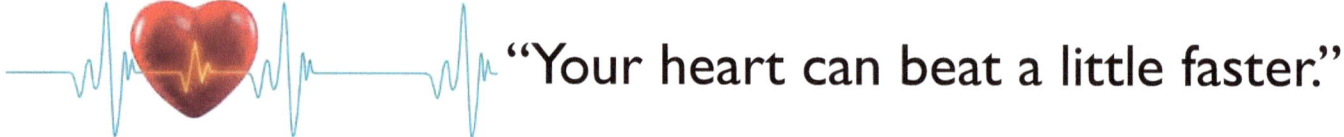 "Your heart can beat a little faster."

"When you look into the person's eyes you don't want to stop," mumbled Alex.

Nonnie smiled, "Yes. And, you might think about kissing or holding the person."

Alex stood up. "Enough talking. I'm going home." he said, and he left.

Tamika looked at Nonnie and shrugged. "He better figure out this crush thing soon, Nonnie," she said. "Cuz I'm getting bored with it!"

That night, Nonnie thought of a way to help Alex.

She called Mr. V. and invited him to her house to make pizza. She made sure Tamika and Alex were there, too.

They had a great time!

Chapter Sixteen: Wanting a Relationship & Love

After they made the pizza, while they waited for it to bake, Nonnie said, "I've been thinking some more about relationships. Is it possible to want a relationship with another person and not have one?"

Tamika said, "I kinda feel like that. I don't have a crush on anyone. But, all my friends are getting boyfriends and girlfriends. What if I want a partner and no one wants to be with me? Will I be left out, Nonnie? Will I be alone?"

Nonnie gave Tamika a hug, and Tamika gave Nonnie a hug right back. Nonnie said, "It can feel like everyone else is happy and that can be hard."

Tamika said, "My mom said it's okay to wait."

Alex grunted. "It might be better to not have a crush. I still don't understand love. How do I figure this out?"

Mr. V. and Nonnie looked at each other. Mr. V. said, "A lot of grown ups try to figure out love, Alex!"

Tamika stepped up to ease her friend's shyness. "How can we know if we're really in love?" she asked.

Nonnie laughed. "There are so many books about that very question, Tamika," she said.

"So it's easy to understand?" Alex asked hopefully.

"No," said Mr. V. and Nonnie together and they grinned.

"When we were young," Nonnie began, nodding at Mr. V. He was younger than Nonnie, but she guessed they had similar experiences. "How did you approach a person you liked?" she asked, still smiling.

Mr. V. said, "I wrote them a note!"

"A note," Alex said, confused.

"Like this," Nonnie said. She pulled a paper and pen from her purse and wrote:

Mr. V. laughed.
Tamika said, "So weird!"

Alex laughed, too, but he secretly thought a note like that might be a good idea.

Nonnie studied Alex, then she said, "Having a crush on someone doesn't mean you're in love, Alex."

"Love is a feeling," said Nonnie. "People describe love differently."

"I have all kinds of feelings," Alex groaned. "What makes love different?"

Tamika stood up and danced around the kitchen. "Like love in the movies. Love at first sight*!" She giggled.

Alex snorted, "Not interested in movie love!"

Nonnie was careful. She was sensitive to Alex's feelings. "How would you describe movie love, Alex?" she asked.

"You know, when two people see each other and BANG, they're in love and ready to die for each other." Alex said.

"Like Romeo and Juliet," sighed Tamika. "Juliet standing on a balcony, waiting for Romeo!"

Alex grinned, "I can't see you waiting on a balcony for anyone or anything, Tamika. You go after what you want."

Tamika smiled, "You're right. I do."

"Ummm," said Nonnie. "So, you don't believe in love at first sight."

Alex said, "I believe I could be attracted to someone at first sight."

Tamika agreed, "Sure. I have crushes on celebrities just because I like the way they look, but I can't really be in love with them. I don't even know them."

Nonnie asked, "To really love someone, do we need to know the person?"

Mr. V. looked at Nonnie. He said, "It's OK to believe in love at first sight. As long as we know the difference between love and attraction."

Alex mumbled, "What if...you're attracted to someone...what if the person says *no*. Like in the notes you two sent when you were kids. What did you do if someone checked *no*."

Mr. V. chuckled. "I felt sad. Then I tried someone else!"

"Me too," Nonnie said. "I felt lonely but I got over it. Things get better."

Tamika thought of one of her friends. "Break ups are hard," she said. "I mean real break ups," she grinned at Nonnie and Mr. V. "Not those weird notes you used!"

Mr. V. laughed. "There are different types of love, too."

Nonnie agreed. "We teach about love. One type of love is friendship love*, like you two have for each other. Another type of love is family love*."

Alex shook his head, "I'm thinking of a love that's different than friendship or family," he said.

Mr. V. knew what Nonnie was thinking. He added, "There is also a mature love* that develops over time."
"Like your great-grandparents," said Tamika.

Alex mumbled, "I don't have time to wait a long while. I need to know now."

Nonnie soothed, "I know you do, Alex. Think about the ways you and Tamika described attraction. Could you be attracted to your crush and not really 'in love' with the person?"

Alex just grunted.

"Love can also be obsessive*," said Mr. V. "Which means a person can be jealous* and possessive*."

Tamika thought about the game they played at the pizza place. "That kind of love doesn't sound healthy," she said.

"It isn't healthy," Nonnie said. "In a healthy relationship, people are safe together. Can you think of ways a person in a relationship could show they were jealous?"

Alex and Tamika looked at each other. Alex said, "We have friends who are together. One of them is really jealous."

Tamika nodded. "There's a lot of phone checking and yelling about texting."

Nonnie said sadly, "Is the jealous person possessive?"

When the children were unsure, Nonnie told them a story about a teen with a jealous partner. The partner controlled the teen's friends and told the teen to lie.

Alex said, "That does sound possessive. It would be good if that relationship ended."

Tamika sighed, "I see people in our school in those kinds of pushy relationships." She frowned. "I think some people confuse attraction and love."

Nonnie agreed. "Two people can be attracted to each other and not be in love. Two people can be in love and not do sexual things."

Alex groaned. "I just want to know if I'M in love….."

Everyone got quiet and Alex's eyes opened wide. He rolled his hands into tight fists. He looked like he was ready to run away. Tamika thought he seemed surprised by his own words!

"It's okay, Alex," she soothed. "It's okay to wonder about love."

Nonnie hugged both the children. "Tamika is right. It is OK, Alex. Being attracted to someone is a new feeling for you."

"Ugh!" Alex said as he turned and left Nonnie's house. "I think we've talked about this enough. I just need to think by myself!"

Chapter Seventeen: Alex's Crush!

Later that night, Alex thought about the person he decided might be his crush. He made a list.

He wrote:

> When I'm with this person, I feel:
>
> Happy. I laugh.
>
> Safe
>
> Like I can be myself

He used a purple marker like Tamika used and thought of her. He felt those things with Tamika, too, but she definitely wasn't his crush. What made this feeling different?

He got out another piece of paper and wrote:

> When I think about this person, I:
>
> Like the way they look
>
> Get butterflies in my stomach
>
> Feel like kissing

He knew! Suddenly, Alex knew the name of his crush!

The next day at school started an important week. Every year, Tamika and Alex's school hosts a big dance. It's called Homecoming and happens the day after the biggest Friday football game of the fall.

Everyone dresses up. Homecoming is a big deal.

Tamika had her dress but she decided she didn't want to go to the dance with just one person, so she was going with a group of friends. She thought about Nonnie and her mom's words. Some day she may want a relationship with someone special. Waiting is okay.

Alex acted like he had a big secret. He wouldn't even share with Tamika. The Monday before the big dance, Alex surprised everyone during lunch!

Kendle was Alex's crush!

Kendle said "Yes," and everyone clapped.

Tamika said, "You even fooled me, Alex, but I should have known. You always wanted to be with Kendle. You have fun together. You like the way she looks. And, you're happy when you're with her! You're attracted to Kendle!"

Alex glared at Tamika, feeling awkward*, but Kendle said, "I feel exactly the same way about you, Alex."

Alex gave Kendle the best smile he'd ever given anyone!

He was very, very happy!

After Alex figured out Kendle was his crush, he and a few friends who were peer educators gathered at the Teen Center to talk about what they'd learned.

As peer educators, they wanted to create games and learning activities to teach their friends.

Kendle asked the group, "What should we teach about kinds of relationships? We should focus on healthy relationships," she said with confidence. David agreed.

Tamika grinned. She asked, "Hey Nonnie, what if we facilitate* the class? We're ready, right Alex?"

Alex smiled, thinking about taking Kendle to Homecoming. He said, "Absolutely!"

Nonnie gave them a big thumbs up!

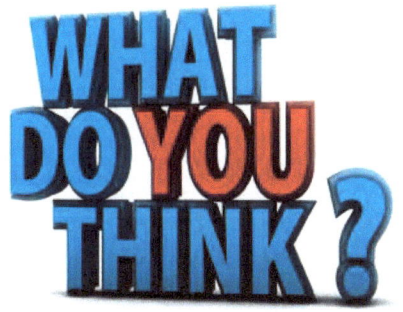

What do YOU Think?

Tamika and Alex learned about many types of relationships!

List one thing you learned about relationships.
Name four different kinds of relationships.
How do you know when you like someone more than friendship? When you're ready, talk with your trusted adult about attraction!

Please draw or write your thoughts here:

Glossary

Abuelito: Tamika's special name for her grandfather. who spoke Spanish.

Admit: In this case, say a person is wrong. Nonnie's employee would not say he was wrong when he didn't do his job well.

Adopted: When children are raised by families to whom they were not born.

At Times: Some of the time. Not always.

Attraction: A feeling one person experiences towards another—mostly physical, and based on how someone looks, how a person feels when together.

Awkward: Causing or feeling embarrassed.

Blended Family: A family that results when two families come together.

Blushed: When some people are embarrassed or feel awkward, their faces may feel flushed or hot, or their skin may pink.

Body to Body Connection: In a relationship, a way to decide physical limits.

Broccoli: A healthy vegetable not all people enjoy.

Bullying; The Olweus Bullying Prevention Program definition of bullying is; Bullying is when someone repeatedly and on purpose says or does mean or hurtful things to another person who has a hard time defending himself or herself.

Butterflies in your Stomach: A slang term for the feeling many people feel when excited, anxious, or attracted to someone.

Caprese Salad: A tomato, mozzarella cheese and fresh basil salad created to honor the flag of Italy. Nonnie likes to feed people.

Casual: In this book, a relationship that is not serious.

Challenging; Requiring effort to get through.

Change: When something is different.

Cheating: Not keeping trust. When someone is unfaithful in a relationship.

Christian: A believer in the teachings of Jesus Christ.

Glossary

Commitment: In this book, making a promise to stay connected in a relationship.

Communication: In this book, Nonnie tells the children this is the foundation of a healthy relationship; the ability to share and listen to one another.

Complicated: Made up of many parts; Nonnie says relationships are complicated because they change often and people change.

Connection: When people intersect and relationships are formed.

Consent: The act of saying "yes" to an activity. A person's "no" must be respected.

Counselor: A trained mental health professional who supports people dealing with depression, social anxiety, trauma, grief and other challenges.

Cousins: A child of one's uncle or aunt.

Crush, Crushing on: Being attracted to someone, with or without contact.

Culinary: About cooking.

Custody: The protective care or guardianship of someone.

Cyberbullying: Bullying that happens online through phones, tablets, or computers.

Dentist: A health care professional who cares for dental (teeth) health.

Difficult: Needing a lot of effort to accomplish or make happen.

Divorce: A legal separation of two married people.

Dominican Republic: A country located on the island of Hispaniola, between the Caribbean Sea and the Atlantic Ocean.

Educational Psychology: A branch of learning that studies children in an educational setting with a focus on theories of development.

Embarrassed: Feeling uneasy, awkward, or anxious.

Employee: Someone who works for another person.

Glossary

Employer: A person who hires others to work in a business or organization.

Facilitate: To make easy; in education, facilitation is a way to encourage discussion and interactive learning.

Faith Leaders: People who lead religions.

Fake Friends: Friends who are not trustworthy and may be hurtful in a relationship.

Family love: The type of love felt among people in a family.

Familiar Stranger: A person we see often but do not interact.

Foster Care: When children are not able to be cared for by a family for any reason, they may be placed in the care of other adults. This fostering situation is typically temporary, but may end in adoption.

Foster Homes: Places where children in foster care are provided with a place to stay, food to eat, support, and parenting.

Friendships: A common relationship where people develop mutual trust and respect.

Friendship Love: The kind of love shared by friends.

Gay: Someone who is attracted, physically or emotionally, to a gender same as self.

Glares: Stares at someone with anger.

Ghosting: When people don't return texts or calls without explaining why.

Grief: Deep sorrow, especially after a death or loss.

Guidelines: Promises and agreements made in a group.

Health Care Provider: A physician, nurse, nurse practitioner, physicians assistant, dentist or any other professional who provides health care.

Healthy: In relationships, connection that supports/respects both people and encourages growth and commitment.

Glossary

Heart to Heart Connection: A type of connection that is emotional or feeling.

Hold Space: To offer the gift of a person's presence to another without advice or judgement. Holding space is often done in silence.

Humor: The ability to laugh—the use of jokes or light-hearted stories to help others laugh and release tension.

Important: Of great value.

Intimacy/Intimate: A feeling of closeness and sharing.

Jealous: Suspicion, mistrust, or envy in a relationship.

Jewish: Describing both a religion (Judaism, adhering to one God) and a culture of people.

Kin: Members of family one creates, not necessarily related by blood.

Lesbian: Women attracted emotionally and physically to other women.

Love: A strong emotion; an intense feeling of deep connection.

Love at First Sight: Some people believe two people can fall in love just be seeing each other. Others believe two people need to get to know each other before they can be in love. Tamika called love at first sight 'movie love' and thinks what people feel is attraction. Alex wasn't sure.

Mature Love: Love when partners are able to be other-directed, committed, and open to growth together.

Mental Note: In this book, Tamika reminds herself to think about something later.

Mentor: Someone who supports, encourages, and teaches another person.

Mind to Mind Connection: Connection in a relationship that includes sharing thoughts and wishes.

Minister: A member of the Christian faith who is a faith leader.

Mistake: Doing something wrong or something a person later regrets.

Model Acceptance: Setting an example of accepting all people.

Glossary

Negative Actions: Behavior that leads to problems.

Obsessive: Overly attentive, unable to give a relationship partner space.

Peer Educators: Young people trained to teach their peers.

Peers: People the same age.

Possessive: Demanding someone's total attention and love.

Presence: Connected to holding space—when one person remains with another during stress.

Racial Profiling: When a person is singled out in a negative way based only on the color of their skin.

Racist, Racism: Racism is when people are judged by the color of their skin or their race. A racist is someone who judges others by the color of their skin or race.

Rectangles: A plane figure with four straight sides and four right angles, especially one with unequal adjacent sides, in contrast to a square.

Relational Aggression: As defined by Rachel Simmons in Odd Girl Out, the hurtful attitude of friends, ex-friends, or casual acquaintances to one another, based on relationships.

Relationships: The way two or more people behave and interact towards one another.

Relationship Counselor: A professional whose job is to guide two people ease tension in a relationship. In this book, Alex's parents sought a marriage counselor when one person was unfaithful.

Role Model: A person who sets an example for others.

Romantic: Relationships typically including love. May or may not include sexual experiences.

Romantic Partner: A sweetheart, person with whom someone is in love, two people who enjoy doing romantic things together.

Glossary

Separated: In a relationship or marriage, when two people no longer remain together.

Serious: When something takes consideration; when a person needs to consider a decision carefully. An important relationship.

Sex Ed: Teaching sexual health.

Sexual: Of or about sex.

Sexy: Feeling attractive or sexual; interested in acting sexual.

Shy: Showing nervousness in front of others.

Sibling: Two or more children of the same parents; a brother or a sister.

Single Parent: A parent who raises a child(ren) alone, without a partner.

Sweetheart: Someone who is loved in a relationship.

Taking the Temperature: In this book, looking at the connections in a relationship.

Therapist: A professional trained to guide someone through trauma or mental health challenges.

Tolerate: Put up with; Nonnie tolerates broccoli.

Trust: Belief that someone is reliable and will be true to a commitment.

Trusted Adults: An adult with whom a child is safe; someone who listens and protects a child.

Unhealthy: In a relationship, when a partner or both partners do not support one another and are damaging to each other.

Unique: One of a kind.

Vulnerable: Easily hurt.

Dr. Mary Jo Podgurski is the founder and director of The Washington Health System Teen Outreach and the Academy for Adolescent Health in Washington, Pa.

She is a nurse, a counselor, a parent, a trainer and speaker, and an educator who is dedicated to serving young people. The Outreach has reached over 250,000 young people since 1988. Check out https://www.healthyteens.com/ for information on the Academy and its programs.

Dr. Mary Jo is certified as a childbirth educator through Lamaze International, as a sexuality educator and a sexuality counselor through AASECT (American Association for Sexuality Educators, Counselors and Therapists) as an Olweus Bullying Prevention Program trainer and through Parents As Teachers. Read more about Dr. Mary Jo at https://www.drmaryjopodgurski.com/

She is an authorized facilitator for the Darkness to Light abuse prevention program. Dr. Mary Jo is the author of the *Ask Mary Jo* weekly column in the *Observer-Reporter* newspaper and answers 6—10 questions from young people daily. She wrote *Nonnie Talks about Gender* as a labor of love in 2014 and The Nonnie Series™ was birthed!

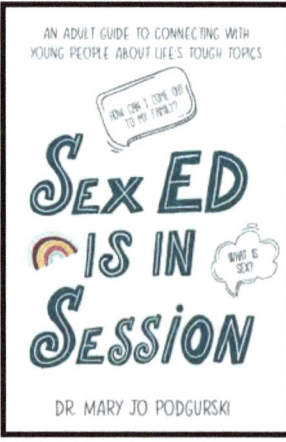

In March 2020 Dr, Mary Jo launched her book for parents and trusted adults through One Idea Press—*Sex Ed is in Session: An Adult Guide for Connecting with Young People about Life's Tough Topics.*

Most importantly, Dr. Mary Jo and her partner Rich are the parents of three wonderful adult children and are blessed to be grandparents. She is a Nonnie in Real Life!

Dr. Mary Jo believes in all young people.

She believes #EachPersonIsAPersonofWorth
Please pass it on.

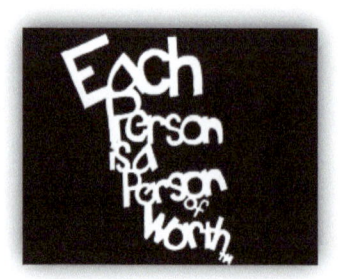

About the Nonnie Series

Writing *Nonnie Talks about Gender* in the summer of 2014 was a true labor of love. The idea of a "Nonnie Series" never entered my mind. The reactions to *Nonnie Talks about Gender* surprised and humbled me. I began to realize gender wasn't the only challenging topic in our world. Social media and 24-hour news have created information overload, where even elementary school children are inundated with potentially confusing and troubling subjects. How should adults open the door to these teachable moments?

As a young nurse I became a birth advocate; as a certified Lamaze childbirth educator I have continued my commitment to birthing women and families since the 1970s. In 1973, I began working with pediatric oncology at Memorial Sloan Kettering Cancer Center in New York City. My passion for birthing normally dovetailed with my growing commitment for death with dignity. I became a hospice nurse in the 1980s. Long before the "circle of life" became part of a popular film for children, I learned how vital birth and death are to the human experience…and how often both topics are avoided when talking with children. With birth and death advocacy as my foundation, I decided to tackle these subjects in books for children as part of a series based on the "Nonnie" concept. Then, life intervened.

As an ally and advocate for racial and social justice, I cannot ignore how much our culture needs to address racial equity. Then, as I was presenting my child abuse prevention program, *Inside Out, Your Body is Amazing Inside and Out and Belongs Only to YOU*, an eight-year-old child told me what #BlackLivesMatter meant to her. We talked, I listened. This little one's very real fear that her own life was less worthy than another's based on the color of her skin was my inspiration for *Nonnie Talks about Race*.

Nonnie Talks about Puberty was born because another child needed it. I began teaching growing up classes called "What's Up as You Grow Up" in 1984. Gender non-conforming children are often confused during puberty; I couldn't find an inclusive resource on growing up, so I wrote one. Empathy is a learned skill. I hope all children will benefit from the book.

I then completed *Nonnie Talks about Pregnancy and Birth* and *Nonnie Talks about Death*. As a sexologist, *Nonnie Talks about Sex…& More*, was a no-brainer for my next book. *Nonnie Talks about Trauma* was written as a direct result to young people's reactions to the Parkland shooting. I tried to offer a balanced approach. The Let's Talk program really happened in our community. *Nonnie Talks about Consent* and *Nonnie Talks about Disability* came from the needs of children and young people today. *Nonnie Talks about Relationships* deals with real life!

If you have any ideas for the "Nonnie Series," or would like to be informed about coming titles, please connect with me at podmj@healthyteens.com.

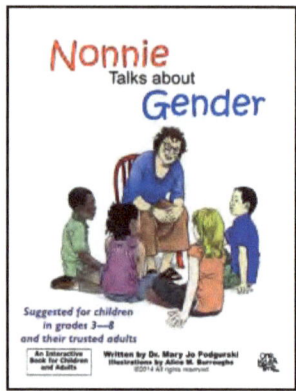
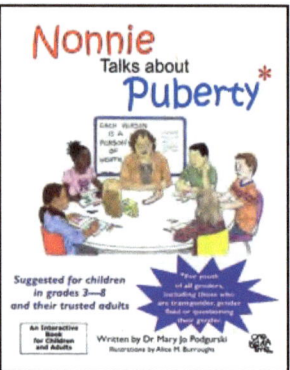
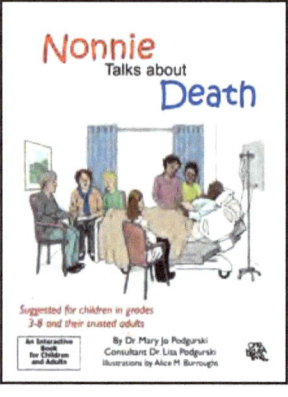

Did you enjoy *Nonnie Talks about Relationships*?
Want to connect with children?
Were you?
Grateful for Nonnie Talks about Quarantine?
Pleased with Nonnie Talks about Disability?
Thankful for *Nonnie Talks about Consent*?
See the need for *Nonnie Talks about Trauma*?
Want to use
Nonnie Talks about Sex…& More
to expand 'the talk' with a young person?
Need *Nonnie Talks about Death* in your life?
Interested in *Nonnie Talks about Puberty*?
Curious about *Nonnie Talks about Race*?
Intrigued by *Nonnie Talks about Pregnancy and Birth*?
Wonder about *Nonnie Talks about Gender*?
Entranced by the concept of the Nonnie Series™?

Dr. Podgurski has dedicated her
life to empowering young people.
She strives to model her motto of
"Each Person is a Person of Worth"
through education, writing, and trainings.
She is available for workshops and consultation.
She is also the author of 34 books.
You can find her books, including the Nonnie Series™,
at Amazon or on her website, drmaryjopodgurski.com

You can reach her at:
Email: podmj@healthyteens.con
http://www.healthyteens.com/
Toll free #: 1 (888) 301-2311

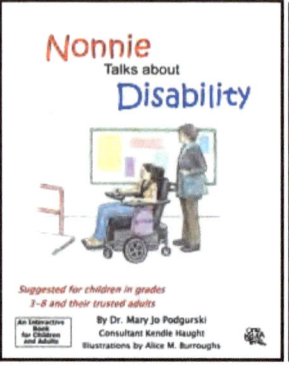

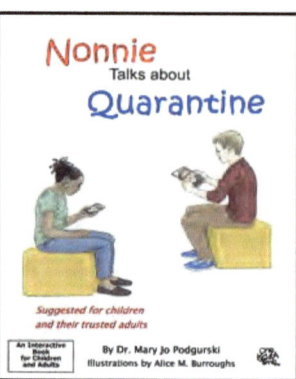

Coming soon….

Nonnie Talks about Mental Health

100

©2020~ All rights reserved   AcademyPress ~ http://www.healthyteens.com/

www.ingramcontent.com/pod-product-compliance
Lightning Source LLC
Chambersburg PA
CBHW041700160426
43191CB00002B/36